France
Classical Art Tours

Versailles

Paolo Cangioli

Translated by Eurolingua, Professional Language Services Ltd,
15-16 Newman Street, Oxford Street, London W1P 3HD

Original title: Versailles

Chief editors of ,,Classical Art Tours'':
Silvio Locatelli und Marcello Boroli

© Manfred Pawlak Verlagsgesellschaft mbH, Herrsching
Distributed in the UK by Hawk Books Ltd

© Instituto Geografico de Agostini SpA, Novara

Versailles, City of Kings

Versailles . . . »the most dreary and barren of places, with no view, no woods, no water and no land . . .«. That was how it was described by one denigrator, the Duc de Saint-Simon, the memoirist. And, indeed, at the beginning of the sixteenth century, one would hardly have expected that within a few decades this marshy area would become the hub of French political and social life. This piece of land, now bleak and almost uninhabited – there was only an old ruined castle, a little church and a handful of houses – was however an excellent hunting ground where the good king Henry IV enjoyed going to relax after the onerous duties of court life.

He was accompanied there in 1607 by his son, the future Louis XIII, who, like his father, was a keen huntsman and often came to Versailles with a few close friends. In 1624, he had what the Venetian ambassador called »a little house« built so that he would not have to return to the Louvre Palace or to his Castle at Saint-Germain-en-Laye at the end of the day. It was more a hunting lodge with twenty-six rooms and a garden of fifty hectares. The cost was modest for a sovereign, ten thousand livres. But the house soon proved too small, so in 1632, the king bought the estate of Versailles and had a real castle built in brick and stone, with extensive gardens and fountains. Completed in 1636, the work cost two hundred and fifty thousand livres, forty thousand of which spent on the gardens alone. It was the first phase of a development which extended the land around the palace to over six thousand six hundred hectares.

Louis XIII died in 1643. When his son, Louis XIV, came to Versailles for the first time, he was only thirteen years old. A passionate huntsman like his father, he returned there a number of times and, when in 1661 he sought a secluded place for his love affair with Louise de la Vallière, he immediately thought of the hunting lodge which was so close to Paris and yet so far from prying eyes. From that moment the fate of Versailles was perhaps sealed, even though it would be many years before it became the permanent seat of the entire court.

There has been much speculation as to what prompted the king to abandon the Paris royal palace, the Louvre: perhaps the wish to build a palace to suit his own tastes, his resentment of the Parisians after his hasty nocturnal flight during the Fronde, his disgust for a city that was dirty and subject to frequent epidemics caused by the »bad air«, his love of nature and fresh air, his passion for hunting, his political need to bridle an undisciplined nobility, or lastly the Machiavellian scheme of bringing about the nobility's financial ruin to keep it at his mercy. Perhaps all were reasons which partially determined him – though none decisively – to move the political and cultural nerve centre of his kingdom to a place twenty kilometres or so from Paris.

In 1661, Louis XIV reigned over the most densely populated nation in Europe, with its twenty five million inhabitants. He was young – only twenty three years old – and his minister, the Italian Cardinal Mazarin, had taught him a love for all forms of beauty: buildings, cloth, marble, jewels and gardens. France was strong and rich and would allow her sovereign to flaunt that wealth in the splendour of his new palace.

The king did not plan however to destroy his father's hunting lodge; so he kept it as the nucleus of the new buildings which would surround and extend it, but without altering even the exterior. In 1662, the construction work began. It was another forty years before the huge architectural feat of the present palace was completed. The architects Le Vau and

Mansart succeeded each other on the building, while Le Nôtre supervised the gardens. But the king also kept a constant eye on the work, sometimes coming up with the ideas himself. Louis followed every stage of the development and had an unerring eye, as is illustrated in an episode described by Saint-Simon. During the building of the Grand Trianon, Louis XIV, accompanied by his customary entourage of courtiers, including the Minister of War, Louvois, noticed that one window was wider than the other. Louvois disagreed, maintaining that all the windows were the same size. As neither the king nor his minister would give in, they decided to measure the windows and it was the king who proved to be right. The difference was negligible, but it existed.

The court soon grew accustomed to coming to Versailles every so often, all the more so because they were able to see quality performances such as Molière's *Tartuffe* in 1664. But the courtiers were so few that the Duke of Enghien wrote that same year that »there are almost no women and very few men«. Four years later, when Louis XIV organised the great entertainment *Les Plaisirs de l'Ile enchantée*, there were already six hundred courtiers.

Before long, their numbers swelled to more than ten thousand. To induce them to stay, the king gave them land for their houses and exempted them from the frequent burdens which befell a nobility constantly assailed by creditors and increasingly falling into debt – in fact he declared that property located inside the royal town would not be subject to confiscation or seizure. This was a brilliant idea which encouraged many people to invest in land around Versailles and quickly resolved the housing problem.

In 1668 there was still a lot of work to be done on the construction of the palace. A painting by Pierre Patel of that year depicts the arrival of the royal procession. As well as a retinue of guards and courtiers on horseback, there is a striking vista of the gardens, with their long avenues, the geometrical designs created by rows of trees and the great fountains, while the palace by comparison seems small, still confined to only a few buildings.

Meanwhile the king wasted no time and was already trying to embellish what was still only a small castle. In the marble courtyard, at the centre of his father's house, he had cages of exotic birds installed. He wanted to refurbish his animal cages with rare beasts and wrote to the Duke of Beaufort, head of the expedition against the Saracen pirates: »I shall send you the appropriate currency to buy me rare animals. I would also like as many birds as you can obtain. I also want oranges.«

Gardens were in fact another of his passions. He had absolute faith in his »gardener«, General Le Nôtre, to whom he gave carte blanche, fully aware how much trust this honest, thrifty and venerable old man deserved. He also planned future expansion, buying in 1668 the little village of Trianon where he would later build a pavilion for rural fêtes. This was replaced by the Trianon de Porcelaine which in turn became Mansart's Trianon de Marbre, the Grand Trianon which can still be seen today.

The park, like the palace, is also more of a renovation than a creation. Louis XIII had planted many trees in 1627, and Boyceau and Menours had laid out the first gardens. Le Nôtre continued their work and had at his disposal a large workforce, huge quantities of water and large areas of land. He was free to create the most beautiful examples of French gardens inspired by the Italian model, notably the Vatican gardens of Belvedere, designed by

Bramante – but he created something original, with terraces, and by varying the patterns of box tree hedges and flower beds. Even paths and avenues are eye-catching with their coloured gravel the grassy lawns alternate with mirror-like lakes; the gardens create a series of movements which espouse the natural contours of the land. There are several different levels, making a smooth transition between the buildings and nature, helping the gaze travel gently from the lines of the palace to those of the flower beds, to rest on the horizon in the distance. There is also the play of the fountains, the liquid patterns of the jets, the great lakes in which the palace is reflected. It is clear why for Le Nôtre gardens were much more than just a beautiful casket for the architectural work – they too were architecture.

The king agreed with his »gardener«. He loved air and light; they were a physical necessity for him. He felt ill at ease, the courtier Dangeau tells us, when a day passed without his going outside in the open air. Although his palace had big windows, inside the air was thick with the throng of courtiers, smelling of the many candles which illuminated the various apartments by day, of the vases brimming with heavily fragrant flowers, of the scent of perfumed water lavishly used by all to cover the stench of rarely washed bodies. In the rooms, the air was the same for months, as the windows remained sealed against the cold with strips of sticky paper from All Saints Day to Easter. No wonder the king needed to go out for a ride or a walk in the open air after the midday meal!

The king wanted these gardens to be magnificant in size, in the quality of the work, and in the rarity and variety of the plants. He particularly sought perfumed species – oranges, lemons, oleander and to protect them he had the huge *Orangerie* built on the sunniest side. The pots holding the palms and citrus fruits were constantly looked after, taken outside and exposed to the sun or brought back inside to protect them from the cold. The king himself was kept informed of the progress of his gardens, of the state of health of his orange trees, even during his military campaigns.

The lakes complete the framework of the gardens; they are vast, like the Pièce d'Eau des Suisses, dug by the Swiss Guard who lost several hundred men due to swamp fever. The largest expanse of water is the Grand Canal, a miniature sea on which a large galley sailed as well as a whole flotilla of gondolas, equipped with a crew of Venetian gondoliers, a gift from the Senate of Venice.

Just as impressive as the château are the gates, with the wide avenues of Sceaux, Paris and Saint-Cloud, which converge at the Place d'Armes and lead through the splendid golden gates to the Cour d'Honneur, continuing on to the Cour Royale where only the privileged few were allowed carriage access.

Still in front of the palace, but at a distance so as not to inconvenience the illustrious guests, rise the majestic horse-shoe shaped buildings of the Royal Stables. The two are rigorously identical, despite the distinction of »Grands« and »Petits« stables. The difference is purely hierarchical, for the former housed the war and saddle horses, and the latter the carriage horses.

Then we come to the palace itself. France had abundant supplies of stone, wood, lime and gypsum. With these materials the main walls were soon built, making a framework of interconnected trusses, between which stone and gypsum were poured. The whole thing was then faced with either marble slabs, ashlar or stucco. Italy had the grandiose monuments of ancient Rome, the recent Renaissance and

Baroque works; Spain had gold and silver; but the young king wanted everything in his palace to be sumptuous. Versailles was to surpass all monuments, ancient and modern, in size and splendour. And so the west facade was to be extended to six hundred and seventy metres, while inside, much of the furniture was of solid silver, even though its artistic value was far greater than that of the metal. The fabrics and tapestries were incredibly lavish. Expense was no object: the brocades in the King's Bedroom alone used several kilos of gold sequins; the orange trees stood in silver pots. There were heavy velvets, silks, carpets from the royal factories, precious marbles everywhere.

This splendour was apparent the moment one entered the palace. Official guests ascended the Escalier des Ambassadeurs – unfortunately pulled down in 1752 – amid a glory of gilt stucco and multicoloured marbles in a geometric design surrounding a bust of the king. But the greatest luxury was reserved for the Hall of Mirrors, a showcase for the skills of the Venetian master glassblowers, and especially for the King's Bedroom, where a solid silver balustrade surrounded the royal bed. Here valets took turns day and night, even when Louis XIV was absent from Versailles, to prevent anyone from slipping through the barrier. When the courtiers walked past the bed, they removed their hats and bowed as if before an altar. The choice of this room's position – at the geometric centre where the directrices of the palace and the avenues converged, the point where the sun's rays first struck, reveals the Sun King's clear desire for self-glorification. He chose the sun as his emblem accompanied by the motto *Nec Pluribus Impar,* and had the sun myth evoked through paintings, sculptures, details of decorative motifs and in the names given to the various salons. These names are all divinities or planets which orbit around the sun: Apollo, Venus, Mercury, Mars. Other salons, like those of Peace and War, reveal the intentions of the man who resorted to the »ultimate right of kings« – the canon – to assert his rights and reign over a glorious and deserved peace. The statues in the garden, too, glorify the beneficent work of the sun which bestows fertility and vitality on the earth.

Pagan divinities did not however cause the »most Christian« to neglect the tribute befitting the king's official religion. A last important addition to the château complex, the Royal Chapel with its cross, dominates the whole of Versailles. Designed in 1699, it was consecrated in 1710, and was built during a particularly difficult time of war, defeats and suffering for the people, and shortages even for the court. And yet, Louis was prepared to spend enormous amounts of money to honour God and the saint to whom the church is consecrated Saint Louis, Louis IX, King of France. Sadly, during the last years of the king's reign, the chapel witnessed a whole series of battles which cast a shadow over the king's old age.

But let us return to happier and more glorious times, when, in 1678, after conquering Flanders and assuring the victorious outcome of the Dutch war, which gave him the Franche Comté, Louis considered Versailles as his permanent residence. Another five years passed before, in May 1682, the king, his ministers and the entire court moved into the new palace. Then the official life of Versailles began.

Etiquette: turn your back on God, but not on the king

... Such were the demands of etiquette. Contrary to general belief, Louis XIV did not invent etiquette, nor did it originate at the court of Spain. This collection of rules, this rigourous timetable became necessary as soon as the court grew beyond a certain size. It already existed in the French court under François I; already in those days the courtiers could find out about the king's movements by consulting a notice – the etiquette – which set out the king's timetable for the day. With Louis XIV, this etiquette was perfected to organise an army of thousands of courtiers who needed to know how and where to move according to the day and the time. And so it was not a mere ceremony but rather a necessary and useful discipline, which lay down boundaries for each and every person, defining the space in which they should move, the clothes which they could and should wear, the actions which were permitted or imposed. In the king's presence you were not allowed to greet anybody; you could not wear a hat without express permission; at mass you had to turn towards the king, even if meant turning your back on the altar; you could not open doors yourself but had to ask an usher; you did not knock on the door but scratched with your fingernail.

There were also rules for dress: only the privileged few could wear the jerkin, the sign of a particular favour from the king; the queen had a train fourteen metres long, the king's daughters ten metres, eight for his nieces, six for princesses of royal blood and only four for duchesses.

Even the chairs had a hierarchical value: princesses of royal blood were entitled to an armchair while duchesses were only allowed a backless stool, the *tabouret*. Nobody could sit down in the presence of the king, not even his brother or his son, without being invited, but that invitation was made in several stages. First, the king would say: »You should sit

down«. A few minutes would go by before he gave the order to bring an armchair; another wait and then at last the order: »Sit down, sir«. At least ten minutes had passed since the first invitation.

Of course relations changed as one descended the hierarchy, and those who were allowed a stool in the presence of the king, were entitled to an armchair in the presence of princesses of the blood – a matter of little interest to the majority of the nobles who had to remain standing most of the day, and only managed to snatch a few moments' rest on the stairs or on the rare seats in the corridors of Versailles.

The nuances of greetings were also dictated in the minutest detail, for everybody. The queen greeted the dukes and duchesses by bowing her head once; a brief nod was sufficient for her close friends of lower rank; for princes of the blood, if she was sitting in an armchair, she had to make a movement as if to rise, without doing so. She stood up only for the king.

Etiquette provided for certain privileges, such as the jerkins already mentioned, but there were other distinctions. One of the most coveted was to be able to obtain a room in the palace, even a poky attic room. Some were granted for a few days, reflecting the degree of royal favour. On the door of the temporarily granted room would be written »de Pompignan«, »Monsieur de Pompignan« or, a supreme favour, »Pour Monsieur de Pompignan«. Louis used these devices to satisfy his nobles vanity at no cost to himself.

Every minute of the day was a pretext for graded distinctions. Officially, until 1789, with the exception of a few alterations to detail, the timetable was rigorously fixed.

In the morning, before his day officially began, the king gave his orders to the chamberlain and to the first gentleman of the bed-chamber; then the doctor entered, the surgeon and the wet-nurse, who gave him a kiss. If the king had slept away from Versailles, he would get into bed. From this moment, the official day had begun.

First on the agenda was the *petit lever*, re-served for a privileged few – members of the royal family, the queen, sons and princes of the blood. The first doctor and the first sur-geon also entered. Louis XIV washed very little, in accordance with the precepts of the medicine of the time, and by contrast to Louis XV. He would wipe his face with a damp cloth, splash his hands with perfumed alcohol, pouring it into a gilt silver dish held by the first valet of the bedchamber, then we would soften them in almond milk and perfume them with extract of jasmine or tuberose which had a strong and lingering scent. He then crossed himself with holy water offered to him by the chamberlain and got out of bed. His brother put his shirt on while two pages put slippers on his feet.

Then the next stage of the *petit lever* began, the »grandes entrées«, restricted to the impor-tant officials of the bedchamber and the ward-robe. With them entered individuals who were necessary but not considered nobles. These so-called »services« were the king's barber, as-sisted by two duty barbers who shaved the king's beard every other day (while Louis XV was shaved every day); the duty pharmacist; the tailor who took orders for the various clothes of the day; the tie-maker who pre-sented the king with a series of cravates knot-ted »Croatian style«; the clockmaker whose duty it was to wind up and set the royal clock to which he held the key; and many other people too numerous to mention here. After the services, the dukes, the ladies and damsels-in-waiting of the queen and princesses of royal blood arrived.

All this time the king sat in his armchair. Next came the readers of the bedchamber, those in charge of the royal entertainment, of walks, lotteries – in other words of amusing the court. Meanwhile the king chose the wigs he would wear that day – at least two. The first, less elaborate and smaller, was reserved for the morning, while the other, piled higher, was for the afternoon. There were also the wigs for important official ceremonies, such as receiving ambassadors and very important guests like the Doge of Genova or the future king of England.

Then the king's shirt was removed. This was no minor event. It was the duty of the master of the wardrobe to slip off the right sleeve while the first valet had to be content with removing the left. While the king was being dressed, the first visitors would arrive, the grand dignitaries of the crown, the prelates, ministers, marshals of France, the grand al-moner, the first architect and a few courtiers honoured with special permission.

Now that the king was dressed, the solemn ceremony of the *grand lever,* which most of the courtiers were allowed to attend, began. After a short prayer, the sovereign left the room and crossed the Hall of Mirrors amid the thronging courtiers who lined his path. Some tried to attract his attention. It was the right moment to ask for favours or present him with written requests, known as placets. On the whole, Louis XIV would not commit himself and replied with the pragmatic »we'll see«; on other occasions he would reply with a »I have never seen him in court« which was the equi-valent of a refusal. He then proceeded to mass.

It would take too long to follow his every move until the time he retired to bed, the *petit coucher*. Let us rather look at three particular moments in the day: luncheon, afternoon strolls and dressing for an official reception.

At around one o'clock, the royal luncheon ceremony took place. Altogether there were one thousand five hundred cooks, meat chefs, pastry chefs and scullery boys to look after the »king's stomach«, supplying meals and refreshements for the entire royal family and for court receptions, and yet there was not one real dining room in the palace. Depending on the occasion, the king would request a solemn meal (the *grand couvert* – served in his apartments), or an ordinary meal (the *petit couvert*), or a limited luncheon (the *très petit couvert*, served in the Salon de l'Oeil de Boeuf, as it was later called). On the days of the *grand couvert* there were fourteen guards in front of his table; another guard accompanied the courtier, whose duty it was to serve drinks to the king, while others had to escort the various dishes as they were borne from the kitchen to the royal table. Anybody who walked past »the king's meats« had to bow, while the soldiers »paid their respects«. During the meal, while »the king's music« played, court gentlemen tasted the dishes before they were presented to the king. These gentlemen ate alone, from gold plates and with gold cutlery – while the sons of France were entitled only to silver gilt – at a separate table, serving themselves with their hands and offering those present the spectable of a legendary appetite. In her letters, the Palatine Princess, the king's niece, listed everything the monarch ate from the numerous dishes presented to him during an ordinary day: »four ladlefuls of various soups, a whole pheasant, a partridge, a large plateful of salad, two large slices of ham, mutton with garlic, a dish of dessert, fruit and four hard-boiled eggs.« There were even days when the king had a bigger appetite and ate much more . . .

Louis XIV wanted rare and costly foods for his table, so the Versailles hothouses supplied him with artichokes in December, peas in May. He was extremely fond of the latter and made them fashionable. Madame de Sévigné wrote to her daughter to tell her that she had managed to eat some, while rich financiers vied with each other to eat the first plate of peas and offered a thousand livres for the first on the market. A thousand livres, when an agricultural labourer earned little more than half a livre a day!

After lunch, the king would go horse-riding or hunting, or walking in his gardens. Now the few who were allowed to follow him were authorised to don their hats with the ritual words: »Your hats, gentlemen!«. Even when he was old, he did not give up these walks, though he had to be pushed in an invalid carriage. He was always accompanied on these walks by Le Nôtre who kept him informed of the progress of the works, suggested new motifs or modifications and listened in turn to Louis XIV's ideas. The latter not only had complete faith in the »gardener«, but also held the man in such great esteem and was so fond of him that he had him carried in a sedan when, despite his eighty years, Le Nôtre remained keen to fulfil the duties of his office: »If only my father could see me, the poor gardener, carried beside the greatest king in the world!« the good man touchingly exclaimed. The king smiled, moved by this spontaneous tribute.

Sometimes there was a great audience in the royal bedchamber, on the occasion of visits from illustrious guests such as foreign sovreigns or ambassadors. On these occasions, Louis XIV, who usually wore clothes of one colour with some gold embroidery and a little lace, displayed the pomp and splendour befitting the greatest sovreign in the world. To receive the Persian ambassador with due ceremony, he wore diamonds worth twelve million over his clothes. At such times, the courtiers too, knowing how to please him, wore all their finery. Madame de Montespan dazzled everybody by wearing »gold on gold, embroidered with gold with golden tassels and was crowned with golden ringlets dressed with gold«, as described by Madame de Sévigné. Even without these costly wonders, we know from the Duc de Saint-Simon that he had to spend forty thousand gold francs on suitable attire for accompanying his wife to the wedding of the Duke of Burgundy and Marie Adelaide of Savoy. But expenditure on clothes was not restricted to these occasions; they frequently had to change wigs, ribbons and shoes according to the dictates of fashion and provide ceremonial or mourning dress for the servants for weddings and funerals. A courtier's pay was not sufficient for all these expenses and to compound matters their administrators took advantage of their absence from their estates to lord it and exploit the situation. All they could do was count on the king's generosity, on a court position, on pensions, the trading of privileges and on gambling, too.

Gambling was another source of revenue, at least for some, although it was often everybody's favourite pastime. Theatrical performances, fireworks, concerts and balls provided pleasant distractions, but gambling remained the most popular entertainment. The king set an example, playing billiards on Monday, Wednesday and Saturday evenings. When the king was playing, distinctions of nobility were temporarily suspended. At Marly, even rich bourgeois were invited and they considered it an honour to lose to the greatest nobles of France. Things did not go that far at Versailles however. Anybody who wished to do so could sit at the various gaming tables and have as their opponent or *partenaire* the queen, the dauphin, the king's brother or even the monarch himself. Meanwhile refreshments were brought round and the king's music accompained the clatter of the die, outbursts of anger, the shouts of the players, and not infrequently their oaths.

There was a choice of games: chess, draughts, dice or cards, of which the latter were the favourite. The fashionable games were faro and *bassetta*, introduced to the court by the Medici ambassador, Bassetti. Calmer people preferred tric-trac, an old variety of backgammon, considered an honest game. But at court games were played which were banned throughout the realm, such as *hoca*, which was punishable by death if played elsewhere. As always, there were some who won, some who lost, and those who tried to assist fortune by cheating (not thought shameful among gentlemen), but even cheating had its limits, as the Marquis of Sessac found out to his cost when he was exiled for cheating against the king.

The winnings and losses were huge. Madame de Montespan lost seven hundred thousand ecus on one Christmas Day; a few years later, the Duchesse de Berry lost one million eight hundred francs to the Portuguese ambassador, at a time when the state revenue amounted to a hundred and sixteen million and the daily wage of a Parisian labourer was no more than one franc. The king would sometimes intervene to save a nobleman from disgrace and would pay the debts of some, bestowing favours and pensions which made certain courtiers increasingly dependent on the sovereign.

At other times there were no losers, only winners, such as when lotteries were held with as many prizes as there were tickets. The king would take a large proportion of them, giving away a great many, and when he won would put the prize back in the game. These prizes were generally jewels, sums of money, or more rarely vases, furniture or carpets from the royal factories.

But sadly life was not all joy and contentment. Wars often broke out, each one longer and costlier than the last. The war of the League of Augustus, which lasted nine years, and above all the war of Spanish Secession, from 1701 to 1714, drained France. Precious metals became increasingly rare; the king sent his golden cutlery and silver furniture to the mint so as to be able to pay his troops.

Then came the terrible cold winters of 1709 and 1710. The water froze on the king's table and he had to authorise the people to cut down the royal forest to keep themselves from dying of cold. Disease struck both rich and poor. In a short time, Louis XIV lost his son, known as the *Grand Dauphin,* and his nephew, who had just become Dauphin in his son's place. Then, on 1st September 1715, the king too died. In accordance with etiquette, an official with a black feather in his hat appeared on the balcony of the Cour de Marbre to announce »The King is dead«, then he spun round, having removed the black feather and replaced it with a white one, and shouted three times: »Long live King Louis XV!«

The new monarch was five and a half years old. A week later, he left Versailles. He returned there officially on 15 June 1722.

Alive again

For seven years, Versailles was ousted from power by the Tuileries Palace in Paris and the place lay dormant, waiting to come to life again. Within a few months, the city that had grown up around the castle was deserted. The astronomic rents dropped and it brought poverty for many of the inhabitants. How happy they were to see the king return! They wanted

to stage a huge firework display to celebrate, but unlike Louis XIV, who loved all kinds of tribute, Louis XV thanked them but refused: many things had changed during those seven years, both people and attitudes. Of course, the new king would continue the old ceremonial. He would fulfil his official obligations conscientiously, he would observe and have others observe the etiquette code, but he would only agree to play the part of sovreign for a few hours a day, after which he wished to be able to dispose of his time freely, to live his private life, which was less restricted and easier. He soon stopped sleeping in the large state bedroom and moved to his private bedroom, which was smaller, more comfortable and less chilly.

The atmosphere inside the palace also changed. The furniture was no longer ostentatious and cumbersome in its splendour, but lighter and more elegant. The actual pieces were smaller, more useful and varied according to their use. As well as the usual commodes, everyday furniture began to appear – gaming tables, embroidery, sewing and knitting tables, side-tables for refreshments; no longer the heavy armchairs but the practical wing chairs; no longer solid silver but precious or prized woods such as cherry wood, lemon-tree, king-wood, rosewood; no longer the sweeping applications of gilt bronze, but light bands emphasising the elegance of the lines even in the furniture destined for the palace salons. The splendid roll-top desk made by Œben and Riesener for the king's study was considered by many to be the most beautiful piece of furniture in the world. In the apartments, the magnificent but icy marble on the walls and floors was replaced by wood panelling and parquet which provided insulation against the cold. The heavy velvets were abandoned in favour of light materials and lively, cheerful patterns. From 1738, the huge apartments were divided into small rooms and, lastly, a dining room was built for the king. Now the royal family had a private life. The minute he had fulfilled his official duties, the king would retire to his rooms. He had his own distillery for liqueurs and perfumes, his own kitchen where he prepared jams and refined meals – for he was an excellent cook – for a few close friends. He moved about the palace with the greatest freedom using secret passages which took him to the queen, to his daughters and to Madame de Pompadour, his official mistress and faithful friend.

The exceptional intimacy between the Duchess of Burgundy and the ageing Louis XIV which entitled her to kiss him in public, to sit on his knee and even to read his letters, became commonplace a few decades later. It did not cause a sensation when Louis XV took his daughters coffee in bed or when he agreed not to send Madame Adelaide to a convent, as was the custom, nor that he allowed jokes in his presence. A page-boy struck the king by mistake, thinking perhaps that he was one of his friends: Louis XV tweaked his ears and smiled.

The royal family was equally informal and used nicknames amongst themselves. Madame Sophie was *Graille* (crow), Madame Louise was *Chiffe* (rag) – kind names in comparison to that of Madame de Pompadour, Maman P... Even the queen had her own private life, almost bourgeois in style: she printed holy pictures, painted and organised concerts for a small group of friends in the august Salon de la Paix. In the evening in her apartments she played cards or dice. There were those who dozed and those who fell asleep. The Cardinal de Luynes woke with a start shouting »Assemble the chapter!« There were also those who took the liberty of joking to the limits of good

manners, like the courtier whom the queen asked what he would do if attacked by enemies: »I would defend your majesty with my life!« »And if they were to force themselves upon me?« »Madam, I would do as the guard dog who for a while tries to defend his master's dinner and then sets to eating it with the others«. A pained smile from the queen, but no repercussions for the over zealous courtier. It would not have been so under Louis XIV had anyone been so bold.

And so the atmosphere was much less oppressive at Versailles, but to the detriment of its prestige. The palace seemed no more than a social centre, an obligatory meeting place for those nobles who, for the purpose of their duties or out of administrative necessity, had to go there for their spell of duty or to obtain permits and privileges. The true nerve centre of France was Paris, where the nobles absenting themselves from their lands preferred to stay.

Paris offered more entertainment, of all kinds and at all levels, with salons where the most prominent writers and intellectuals of the day shone. In comparison, Versailles appeared to be merely the king's residence, the place where the wealth produced by the rest of the kingdom was squandered.

With the death of Louis XV, in 1774, and the advent of his nephew Louis XVI, this state of affairs was even more pronounced. There were few changes in the palace, expect for the furniture. One of the new sovreign's first decisions concerned the splendid commode made by Gaudreaux in 1739 for the king's bedroom, which he replaced with a chest of more sober design, in the neoclassic style. The king had a library built, and a blacksmith's, a clockmaker's and an armourer's workshop fitted out, where he carried out experiments in physics and tested the latest weapons. He approved and perhaps perfected the gun which served the armies of the Revolution and of the Empire. Other internal alterations improved hygiene; the »business chairs« – little seats with a receptacle for answering the call of nature – were abandoned in favour of English style water closets with bathtubs in the various apartments. Personal hygiene became a fashion and a necessity.

The most important alterations were to the gardens. No longer rows of cultivated plants laid out in rigorous geometric patterns, but tall trees left to grow freely, the same sort of garden that is found today at Versailles.

Meanwhile, life at the court went on, increasingly becoming a meaningless display. As soon as he could, the king would lock himself up in his workshops, while the queen withdrew to her private apartments to »make music«, sing arias by Grétry or Gluck, read or laugh with her friends. She found it hard to accept the restrictions imposed by etiquette – especially at first – seeing them as irritating, fastidious and pointless rites.

The moment she had the opportunity, the queen simplified these rules, at the cost of upsetting those whose official duty was to serve. Why ask the first chambermaid for a glass of water when it was easier to serve oneself? Why did she have to go out only accompanied by the ladies-in-waiting when it was simpler to do so escorted by a valet? All reasonable innovations which aroused jealousy, resentment – and soon lies.

Although the queen tried to use the services of the domestic staff as little as possible, the number of servants was not reduced. On the contrary, there were even more than before, as can be seen from the fat, hundred and sixty five page *Almanach de Versailles* which lists all the domestic staff, from the presenter of the *Gazette de France* to the king, the queen and the royal family, to the »Captain of the mule-drivers«, when everybody knew that there had not been any mules in the royal stables for years. It was all unnecessary expenditure which further burdened an already ailing purse.

But it was not so much these unnecessary positions or the general wastefulness (the candles were changed every day, even if they had not been lit) which caused a stir over the queen's extravagance. She was reproached for withdrawing to the Petit Trianon, completed in 1768 by Madame Du Barry and acquired by the king for his personal use. »It is for the king's favourite, and so it is fitting for you to have it«, her husband had gallantly replied when he gave it to Marie-Antoinette. Inside, she had a little theatre built where she would perform in front of a few intimate companions. The king had to ask to be invited. But above all, she was reproached for building a small village in a corner of the Petit Trianon, the Hameau de la Reine, comprising a few rustic houses around a little lake. Here, Marie-Antoinette deluded herself that she lived the natural, simple life of a peasant girl which had become fashionable with Jean-Jacques Rousseau. There was a cowshed with cows decked out in ribbons, a sheepfold with perfumed sheep and lambs, a watermill with its wheel that ground nothing, the queen's house where Marie-Antoinette played tric-trac or billiards. Gossiped about, exaggerated, distorted, these costly whims only increased the people's discontent, which exploded when the famine made itself felt. Everybody repeated the thoughtless words of one of the queen's friends: »They haven't any bread? Let them eat cake!« It was 1789, and Versailles was in its final years, the most tragic it had known as the official residence of the Bourbons: on the 2nd May, the king had the deputies of the States

General presented to him in the Salon d'Hercule; on the 6th October, the Parisian mob invaded the palace and escorted the royal family back to Paris.

Then began the dark years of the French Revolution. There were those who wanted to raze the palace to the ground, as the Bastille had been, like the Château of Marly-le-Roi which was pulled down. The decisive intervention of the Versailles troops prevented this disaster. The revolutionary government contented itself with auctioning off the royal furniture which was bought mainly by the rich English. A century and a half later, many of their descendants donated the pieces to France, making it possible to restore the apartments with the original furniture.

After the stormy Revolution, Versailles lay dormant once more, but the palace came to life again with a few illustrious guests. On 3 January 1803, Pius VII appeared on the balcony of the Hall of Mirrors to bless the crowd assembled in the gardens. Napoleon I intended to restore and revive the Grand Trianon. Louis Philippe, King of the French, tried to resuscitate Versailles by staying there for short periods with his family, but with little success.

In the years which followed Versailles hosted various guests, some more welcome than others. In 1855, Queen Victoria of England; in 1871 Kaiser Wilhelm I of Germany, who was actually crowned in the Hall of Mirrors; the National Assembly during the Commune; the French Parliament for the presidential elections; and on 18th June 1919 it hosted the signing of the Treaty of Versailles which ended the First World War.

Recent years have seen the palace of Versailles restored. A decree by the French Government in 1957 ensured the return of all masterpieces that were on French soil. Many French and foreign foundations have made donations and are still contributing to the restoration of the palace rooms to their former splendour. It is a delicate operation requiring time, money and skill. It took at least twenty years to restore the Queen's Bedroom alone and it will take another twenty to bring Versailles back to its full glory. When the work is finally completed, the world will have retrieved part of its great artistic and cultural heritage.

Marble bust of Louis XIV, sculpted by Antoine Coysevox
(Château of Versailles, the Salle du Grand Couvert).

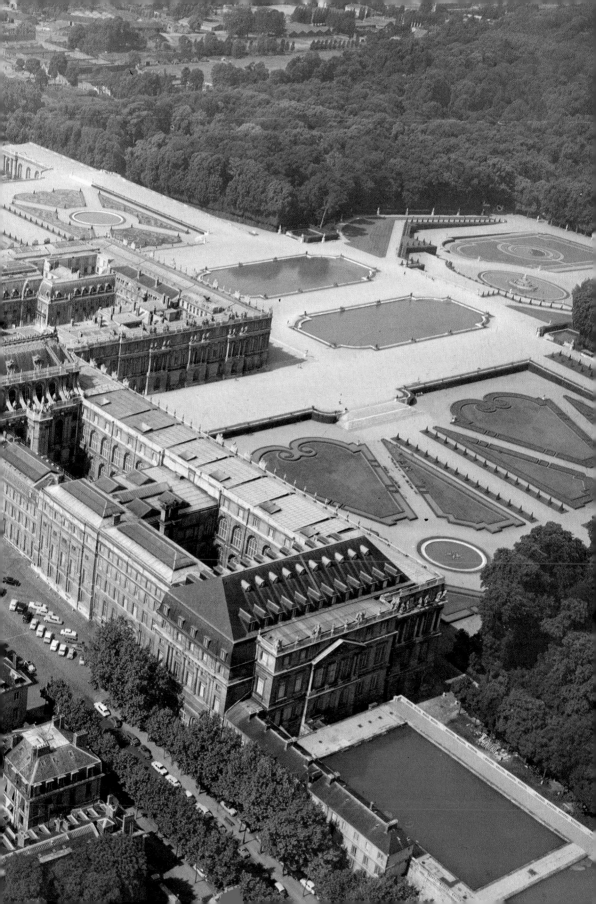

The Evolution of Versailles

The original nucleus of the Château of Versailles was a hunting
lodge built by Louis XIII in 1624 and extended between 1631
and 1634. The U-shaped palace, of stone and brick, designed
by Philibert Le Roy, was built around the so-called Cour de
Marbre. On the fourth side it was closed off by a series of high
arches supporting a terrace. The subsequent modifications were
carried out by Louis XIV in 1662, when, after the death of
Mazarin (1661), the king assumed full power. The Sun King
appointed Louis Le Vau to supervise the works and he added
four corner pavilions at the vertices of the palace and two
imposing outbuildings enclosing a new courtyard, the Cour
Royale. In front of this Le Vau made a circular piazza with
surrounding walls culminating in two obelisks; this stage of the
building was documented in the picture opposite by Pierre
Patel (1668, Château of Versailles National Museum). Even
then, the palace soon proved too small for the king's
requirements and in 1669 he asked Le Vau to envelop the
existing building in a new, bigger, stone structure, the Château
Neuf, which had a facade overlooking the gardens made up of
two front wings joined by a long arcade supporting a terrace. A
final extension was required by Louis XIV when he transferred
the seat of the court and the government to Versailles in 1678.
Jules Hardouin-Mansart was commissioned to add two long
wings to extend the palace laterally (the northern Aile Neuve
and the Aile des Princes to the south), and two other wings, the
Ailes des Ministres, extending the other way towards the city,
creating a new courtyard, the Cour des Ministres. In the
foreground, towards the garden, Mansart closed off Le Vau's
terrace with the long Hall of Mirrors. The Château of Versailles
now looked much as it does today (shown on the previous
pages). The only difference is the construction of the Opéra at
the end of the Aile Neuve by Jean-Jacques Gabriel and the
rebuilding of the northern pavilion of the Cour Royale by the
same architect. Its counterpart on the other side of the
courtyard was built by Dufour in 1829.

The painting at the top of the opposite page is the work of an anonymous artist in 1675 (Château of Versailles National Museum). It depicts the facade overlooking the park, designed by Le Vau and completed, after the architect's death, by François d'Obray. Note the long terrace over the arcade which was later closed by Mansart when he built the Hall of Mirrors. Bottom left, a painting by Pierre Denis Martin dated 1722 shows the facade looking out at the city after Mansart's alterations (Château of Versailles National Museum).

Above, the Cour de Marbre, so called because of the marble paving stones. The surrounding buildings date back to the time of Louis XIII and represent the oldest part of the palace, even though they were subsequently altered and embellished: the marble columns, the roof balustrades with statues and vases, the carved busts on the corbels between the windows, among other things, were added by Le Vau and Mansart to make the older building blend in with the style of the new château. The windows of Louis XIV's bedroom open onto the courtyard.

The Grands Appartements

The Grands Appartements proper are those located in the two lateral buildings of the Château Neuf which Le Vau built around Louis XIII's original hunting lodge. Reserved for the king (in the north wing) and the queen (in the south wing), they became known as the Grands Appartements during the time of Louis XV to distinguish the state rooms from the private quarters, known as the Petits Appartements. The king's Grand Appartement, looking out over the Parterres du Nord, was originally reached via a wide staircase from the Cour Royale, the Ambassadors' Staircase, built by François d'Obray from plans by Le Vau and sadly destroyed in 1752. Today, access is through the Salon d'Hercule (opposite page, top), a grandiose room linking the old part of the palace and Mansart's new wing. Built by Robert de Cotte between 1712 and 1736, it is decorated with marble, gilt bronze and valuable paintings including the large ceiling fresco by François Lemoyne depicting the *Apotheosis of Hercules*, 1733–1736 (opposite page, bottom). Beyond this salon is a suite of six rooms. Except for the first (built by Mansart and famous as the Salon de l'Abondance) they were all by Le Vau and each one was named after a planet: Venus, Diana, Mars, Mercury and lastly Apollo, the Sun (Louis XIV's emblem), to which the whole iconography of Versailles is devoted. Opposite the king's Grand Appartement, overlooking the Parterres du Midi, is the queen's Grand Appartement, also designed by Le Vau but subsequently much altered. The sweeping marble staircase built by Mansart between 1679 and 1681 leads to the Queen's Guards' Room, then to the Queen's Antechamber or the Salle du Grand Couvert, the Salon des Nobles and the Queen's Bedroom. The Grands Appartements was the term used to describe all the rooms reserved for the sovereign's public life, including the Hall of Mirrors with the adjacent Salons of peace and war, and the King's Apartment, created by Mansart in the central section of the Vieux Château and comprising five rooms: the King's Guards' Room, the King's Antechamber, the Salon de l'Oeil-de-Boeuf, Louis XIV's Bedroom and the Council Chamber.

Opposite, the Salon de l'Abondance, built by Mansart. During Louis XIV's time, it served as an antechamber to the famous Cabinet des Medailles where the Sun King kept his collections of valuable objects. Under Louis XVI, it became the king's gaming room. Sadly, there is almost nothing left of the original furniture, which we know from various sources to have been very elaborate, with many pieces of chased silver, such as tables, chairs and candelabra, designed by Le Brun. These were later melted down to make coins during a period of economic hardship.

Above, a detail from the Salon de Venus, with the statue of Louis XIV, by Jean Warin. The Salon, which served as an entrance hall, is a typical example of Le Brun's decorative style, especially the wall panelling of brightly coloured marble influenced by Roman style which was his hallmark. To obtain the valuable stone, rare in French architecture before Louis XIV, the king reopened the quarries in the Pyrenees which had been closed since the fall of the Roman Empire.

Left, the Salon de Diane, the second entrance hall of the king's Grand Appartement, decorated with themes related to hunting and navigation, two activities over which the goddess presided. The ceiling fresco was painted by Charles de la Fosse and Claude Audran. The different scenes are framed or surrounded by a variety of sumptuous gilt stuccoes, a typical seventeent century decorative technique. Only in the next century did the fashion for a more refined, uniform composition spread.

Above, detail from the ceiling of the Salon de Mars, former ballroom and concert hall. Overleaf, the Salon de Mercure, Louis XIV's bedroom before the king moved to the room in the centre of the Vieux Château. The room is a major example of Le Brun's skill in furnishing and decorating the rooms of Versailles. The artist supervised everything himself down to the minutest detail, so as to obtain a perfectly harmonious result. He himself then executed a few of the decorations while he entrusted other details to his collaborators, such as the stuccoes, mostly the work of Regnaudin and the Marsy brothers. Le Brun often commissioned the tapestries from the Gobelins factory.

PRISE DE LA VILLE DE L'ISLE
EN FLANDRES PAR L'ARMÉE DV
ROY LOVIS XIV. COMMANDÉE
PAR SA MAIESTÉ EN PERSONNE
EN L'ANNÉE M.DC.LXVII.

Below, the central ceiling medallion of the Salon d'Apollon, one of the rooms in the king's Grand Appartement. Every decorative detail is related to the sun myth, designed to glorify Louis XIV. Executed by Charles de la Fosse, the ceiling paintings are framed by elaborate gilt stuccoes. In the centre, the artist has depicted the sun in his chariot surrounded by allegorical figures. A skilful colourist and orchestrator of figures and crowds, La Fosse exercised strict formal rigour in controlling the overall lavishness.

Below, a figure from the Salon de la Guerre. The wall above the fireplace is dominated by the imposing oval depicting a triumphant Louis XIV, a stucco bas-relief in which Antoine Coysevox has painted the monarch on horseback trampling on his enemies. The ceiling, shown overleaf, represents the allegorical figure of France in the centre, and in the surrounding semi-circular panels her subject countries. It is the work of Charles Le Brun, the king's favourite painter and great exponent of the artistic splendour and political prestige of the France of the Sun King.

Below, the famous Hall of Mirrors which, with the Salons of War and Peace at either end, was the setting for lavish feasts and solemn audiences. Seventy-three metres long, it takes its name from the mirrors which line the seventeen arches facing the windows. The space is admirably broken up by red marble pillars with gilt bronze capitals, niches with classical statues, chased trophies and elegant female statues of gilded wood holding cornucopias with candelabra of rock crystal (right). The ceiling frescoes are the work of Le Brun.

Left, Louis XIV's bed in the King's Bedroom, which was the central room in the Vieux Château and was only used as a bedroom from 1701. The decoration of the room represents a major stylistic development, the ceiling's sober gilt decoration on a white background and the elegant gold and white wood panelling marking the transition from Baroque pomp to eighteenth-century elegance. The alcove, above which is a high-relief by Nicolas Coustou depicting France watching over the king's slumber, is separated from the rest of the room by a solid silver balustrade. The bed, a copy of the original, has curtains of gold and silver brocade. In this room the ceremony of the lever du roi took place every morning. The king's family and courtiers waited to be admitted in the adjacent Salon de l'Oeil de Boeuf (opposite, top), a room which owes its name to the oval window in the great gilt stucco frieze around the base of the ceiling. A detail from the frieze (opposite page, bottom) shows infants and cherubs playing music, dancing, playing and taming wild animals.

This painting by Jean Nocret with the royal family portrayed as Olympian deities occupies a wall of the Salon de l'Oeil-de-Boeuf. Louis XIV, with the sceptre, is seated on the right, beside his wife, Marie-Thérèse, surrounded by his children; to the king's right, is his mother, Anne of Austria, while to the far left we recognize the king's younger brother, Philippe. The representation of the monarch as the supreme Olympian god is fully in keeping with the pomp and splendour of the palace at Versailles, the object of which was to glorify Louis XIV. Versailles epitomises an era, and is the visible and concrete expression of the concept of monarchy as absolute power, the source and focal point of all life forces. It was no coincidence that the king chose as his emblem the sun which »for the unique splendour that surrounds it, for the light it sheds on the other stars which form around it a kind of Court . . . for its constant and immutable path . . . is surely the most beautiful and most vivid image for a great sovereign.«

In the queen's Grand Appartement, the principal room was the
bedroom (left) where the sons of the king of France came into
the world. Le Brun's original decoration was entirely changed
by Maria Leczinska, Louis XV's wife, between 1730 and 1735.
During this period the gilt ceiling with Boucher's medallions and
the precious wood panelling by Verbeckt in pure rocaille style
were fashionable again. Marie-Antoinette made a few changes
to the room, including the magnificent delicately coloured
brocade panels (see detail).

Below, the Salon des Nobles, the queen's official reception room. Of the original decoration only the allegorical paintings on the ceiling by Michel Corneille remain. The mirrors, the wood panelling, the tapestries of apple green damask, the blue marble fireplace, Riesener's corner tables and commodes with gilt bronzes by Gouthière date back to Marie-Antoinette. Opposite, the Queen's Antechamber or the Salle du Grand Couvert, which is decorated with four Gobelins tapestries depicting Louis XIV's exploits.

The walls of the Queen's Guards' Room (below), decorated with mythological paintings by Noël Coypel, are covered with geometrical relief patterns in precious marble, like the chased metal and gilt bas-reliefs of the Louis XIV period. The same geometrical designs appear on the Queen's Staircase or the Marble Staircase (opposite), which was the counterpart of the Ambassadors' Staircase, no longer in existence. The coloured marble decoration is enhanced by a trompe-l'oeil painting creating the illusion of more space.

The Royal Chapel (opposite), consecrated in 1710 to Saint Louis, is on two levels: the upper level, for the king and the royal family, has a high Corinthian colonnade, while the lower level pillars are more solid with stucco decorations. The harmonious lines and the lavish decor make this building a masterpiece of Baroque classicism. The organ case was designed by Robert de Cotte. Below is a detail showing King David playing the harp.

The Petits Appartements

The Petits Appartements, thus named for their »private«
character, are on the first floor of the palace and look out over
the Cour de Marbre. These are the Cabinets Intérieurs,
accessible only to a privileged few, mainly art lovers, where
Louis XIV kept the masterpieces of his collections: famous
paintings such as Leonardo da Vinci's *Mona Lisa* or
Giorgione's *Concerto Campestre*, medals, crown jewels,
objects of crystal or precious stones, new exhibited in the
Louvre. In 1738, Louis XV commissioned Gabriel to rearrange
these rooms completely to make them into a truly private
residence. As well as his bedroom (right), decorated with
carved gilt panelling by Verbeckt and enhanced by a
magnificent commode made in 1739 by Gaudreaux, there are
reading rooms, drawing rooms, dining rooms where the king
ate on his return from hunting, kitchens where the king himself
sometimes liked to cook, and large aviaries. For her part, the
queen, Maria Leczinska, arranged the drawing rooms where
her entourage used to gather as befitted their confident and
refined taste. The Petits Appartements are one of the best
examples of Rococo style. The stately solemnity of Louis XIV's
style is replaced by softer, more elegant lines and less
cumbersome ornamentation such as garlands, spirals of flowers
and leaves, ribbons, festoons and bows. The Louis XV style,
rich in admirable examples of all the decorative arts, was best
expressed in the furniture. Created for smaller rooms and
suitable for a less restricted private life, it was designed
according to more functional criteria. In the rooms, marble
gave way to wood panelling on the walls and parquet flooring
which provided more efficient protection against the cold. The
heavy velvets were replaced by delicately coloured shimmering
silks with vivid patterns, and the gilt bronze decorations
became light and sinewy like climbing creepers. Few alterations
were made by Louis XVI, who was content to add his
workshops, an observatory and an elegant library where he
could indulge his love of reading. Marie-Antoinette introduced
decorations inspired by recent archaeological finds, especially
those of Herculaneum and Pompeii.

The Salle de la Pendule (below) was named after the astronomical clock that was installed there in 1754. The mechanism, designed by Passement and executed by Dauthiau is enclosed in a magnificent chased bronze case made by Caffieri. The clock showed not only the hour, but also the day and the month, the lunar phases and the positions of the planets in the solar system. In the centre of the room is the model of Bouchardon's statue of Louis XV on horseback, which originally stood in the Paris square dedicated to the king (now Place de la Concorde) but was removed in 1792.

Right, the precious roll-top writing desk from Louis XV's study. The inventor of the elaborate mechanism – a slatted wooden panel which could be rolled down to cover the writing surface – and of the decoration, finished off by Riesener, was the cabinet maker Œben. Of harmonious proportions, with precious inlaid panels of subtly coloured woods enhanced with gilt bronze foliage and whirls, this writing desk is a masterpiece of rococo cabinet making.

On the opposite page, top, Louis XV's private dining room, where he would eat on his return from hunting. Redecorated between 1754 and 1755 the walls are wood panelled. The purity and sobriety of the lines heralds the Louis XVI style. An impressive pendulum clock against one wall catches the eye. This was made by Berthoud, while, the sumptuous ebony case, surmounted by a gilt bronze sculpture of Apollo in his chariot, is the work of Balthazar Lieutard. The room is reached via the Antichambre des Chiens (bottom left), which is decorated in elegant stucco with animal motifs and hunting scenes, and with painted medallions depicting flowers and fruits (detail, top right). It is here that the staircase linking the Petits Appartements to the Cour de Marbre culminates. Bottom right, one of the seven bathrooms that Louis XV had built at Versailles. The wood panelling is embellished with gilt medallions celebrating the pleasures of water.

53

Left, the Méridienne, a small room where the queen used to take her afternoon nap. Completed in 1781, it has exquisite wood panelling with decorations of flower shoots, and chairs of gilded wood with draped blue taffeta backs to match the curtains. Below, the Royal Opera, built by Gabriel and Arnoult between 1768 and 1770. The truncated oval design ensures a perfect view, and the acoustics are equally exceptional due to the exclusive use of wood, which is even used to imitate green and pink marble on the walls.

The Gardens

The gardens of Versailles were laid out by Le Nôtre between 1661 and 1668. They are a splendid example of gardens in the French style and were the model for other European palaces. Influenced by the Italian Baroque garden, Le Nôtre created a grandiose and vast complex in which every element was part of a rigorous system, designed to achieve maximum panoramic and scenic effect. The avenues, flower beds, terraces, pools and fountains were arranged according to criteria of order and symmetry in a system which aimed at a global rationalisation of the landscape from the lowest to the highest viewing level: hence the need for perfectly even ground which meant that La Nôtre had to carry out major works to modify the natural landscapes, although a few slopes were incorporated in the layout to create a series of terraces on different levels, joined by flights of steps or long ramps. He set out main avenues running lengthways with minor avenues cutting across them. The precise geometric forms to which the trees and hedges were made to conform is a triumph of art over nature. Flowers were used to provide colour, while water was an important natural element: huge decorative lakes mirror the architecture and the landscape, and the astonishing play of the fountains adds a further dimension. In front of the main body of the château stretches the terrace leading down to the two lakes called *parterres d'eau,* ornamented with magnificent bronze statues depicting the allegories of the rivers (right, the Rodano). Proceeding to the right, past the Parterres du Nord, you reach the Allée d'Eau which leads past the Bassin du Dragon to the Bassin de Neptune. On the other side are the Parterres du Midi, which descend to the Orangerie and to the Pièce d'Eau des Suisses. Alternatively, walking down the central avenue, you come to the *parterres d'eau* and steps lead to the Bassin de Latona, one of most beautiful fountains of Versailles, and to the long lawns known as the »tapis vert«, the green carpet, at the end of which is the *Bassin d'Apollon* and beyond this the Grand Canal more than one kilometer in length.

The Orangerie (top left), made up of three long galleries, with a facade broken up by arched windows, was built under Louis XIV between 1684 and 1686 in the sunniest part of the garden to protect the fragrant orange, lemon and pomegranate trees during the winter. Further to the south, a terrace overlooks the Pièce d'Eau des Suisses (bottom left). This vast lake, dug out by the Swiss Guard between 1678 and 1682, draws the eye beyond the gardens to the horizon in the distance.

From the Parterres du Nord, past the elegant Fontaine des

Pyramides and the Allée d'Eau, an avenue flanked by twenty-two fountains, you reach the elegant Bassin du Dragon (above), one of the many fountains with mythological sculptures which add to the charm of the gardens. The name derives from the sea monster in the centre, wounded by the arrows shot by the children riding on the backs of the swans. Beyond the Bassin du Dragon is the larger Bassin de Neptune, semicircular in shape with statues by Adam, Lemoyne and Bouchardon, and ninety-nine jets of water.

On the opposite page, the Sun's horses, being groomed by Tritons, a marble group by Marsy and Guérin which was in the Grotte des Téthys ornamenting the grove of the Bain d'Apollon, designed in 1778 specifically to house the statue. The picturesque grove is a testimony to the evolution of landscaping art at the end of the eighteenth century and differs from the sculpture of Louis XIV's time, characterised by a measured classicism typical of the French Baroque. Nearby is the Bassin de Cérès or Summer (below), with a group in lead by Regnaudin.

*On the opposite page, a cupid from the Bassin des Fleurs or
Spring. Below, the statue of Bacchus at the centre of another of
the same name, also called the Bassin d'Automne. Le Brun and
his collaborators took their inspiration for the sculptures of the
Versailles gardens from the* Iconologia *by the Italian Cesare
Ripa, a work rich in symbols and allegory, developing an
emblematic cycle of the Sun King-Apollo which corresponds to a
precise celebratory scheme. From this sprang the whole gamut of
gods, nymphs, heroes and allegorical figures which adorn the
huge park.*

*In the Bassin d'Encelade (below), rocks rise out of the water
representing the mountains under which Jove buried the Titan
whose hands and head, reminiscent of Laocoön, are emerging.
From his mouth, open in a cry, springs a jet of water, while
others gush from every side. Although there was no shortage of
water at Versailles, there were so many lakes, fountains,
waterfalls and jets that it was necessary to bring water from the
nearby ponds via a network of pipes and canals, and finally to
draw water from the Seine to fill the reservoirs.*

*It was Girardon who sculpted the statue of Saturn (opposite)
which rises from the centre of the Bassin de Saturne, also known
as the Bassin d'Hiver. He was one of the most rigorous
exponents of the academic classicism proposed by Colbert and
Le Brun. However, as in other famous groups sculpted for the
gardens at Versailles – The Kidnapping of Persephone, Apollo
with the Nymphs – the suggestion of Greek sculpture, apparent
in the modelling, in the gentle treatment of the material and in
the serpentine lines, is tempered by the sensitivity and fineness of
the execution.*

Along the main axis of the gardens, beyond the »green carpet« which starts from the Bassin de Latona, is the Bassin d'Apollon, a vast octagonal mirror of water. At the centre is the magnificent group, sculpted by Tufy, depicting the king of the sun emerging from the water in his carriage to begin his journey across the firmament. Around him tritons and dolphins herald another new dawn. Beyond the Bassin d'Apollon, is the Grand Canal, which during court feasts was full of gondolas, a gift to the Sun King from the Republic of Venice.

The Grand Trianon and the Petit Trianon

In 1668, Louis XIV decided to extend the palace and bought the little village of Trianon on the outskirts of Versailles. He then instructed his architect, Le Vau, to build a pavilion reserved for the entertainment and the repose of the king, far from the pomp of Versailles. That was how the Trianon de Porcelaine was created in 1670, a small building hidden in the woods, its facades covered in blue and white tiles, in keeping with the prevailing fashion for Chinese porcelain. It was replaced in 1678 by the present Grand Trianon (right). Created by Jules Hardouin-Mansart, it is a one-storey building composed of two lateral wings joined by a peristyle, with white and pink marble facades divided by wide arched pillars. Perpendicular to the right wing is a long gallery. This building, like the rest of Versailles, is typical of French Baroque classicism, characterised by an ideal of order and rationality and taking its inspiration from antiquity. It uses the classical architectural and sculptural elements to organise structures and surfaces which are not classical in dimension or grandiosity. From the peristyle, an elegant loggia devised by Louis XIV himself, who imposed it on his architects, one descends to the delightful garden, designed by Le Nôtre on a scale deliberately reduced by comparison with the park of the château. The sparseness of the architectural and sculptural decoration and the respect for the natural elements herald the new eighteenth-century trend in landscape art. To the north-east of the Grand Trianon is the Petit Trianon, a little palace built by Gabriel in 1772 for Louis XV, who spent a lot of time there devoting himself to exotic plants grown in the nearby botanical garden. This little palace, which for its harmonious proportions and exquisite decoration is among the masterpieces of Neoclassical architecture, was given to Marie-Antoinette by Louis XVI. In the gardens, which the queen had laid out according to the fashion for the picturesque that was in vogue at the time, are dotted Neoclassical buildings like the Temple of Love, the Belvedere, and the famous Hameau, a little village with rustic houses. It was in this charming setting, far from etiquette and the conditions of court life, that Marie-Antoinette loved to play the shepherdess.

The apartments of the Grand Trianon, stripped of their furniture during the Revolution, were furnished in Napoleonic style: for example the King's Bedroom (opposite page, top left), which was originally Louis XIV's and then passed on to the Empress Marie-Louise, is clearly Empire style, as can be seen particularly from the magnificent marble-topped rectangular table with legs in the shape of caryatids inspired by strict classicism. In the Emperor's Bedroom (opposite page, bottom left), the square bed and chairs give the room a cold dignity. The Salon des Glaces (left), situated like the King's Bedroom, in the left wing, served Louis XIV as a Council Chamber. It was the Sun King who had the large mirrors and delicate wood panelling put it. Marie-Louise furnished it with numerous little writing desks, pedestal tables and work tables typifying the style of the times with their geometric simplicity of form, their X-shaped legs joined by a thin gilt bronze bar, sabre legs and lyre-shaped sides.

Below, the side of the Petit Trianon, which looks out over the French Garden. The simple facade, made elegant and harmonious by the projecting front of Corinthian pillars and the steps which descend to the formal flower garden, has large French windows. Behind the central windows is the main dining room (opposite page, bottom). Here the decoration – paintings depicting Hunting, Fishing, Harvest and Grape Harvest, and wood panelling with motifs of fruit and festive garlands – evoke the pleasures of the table. Opposite page, top: The Grand Salon, or Music Room.

In the romantic setting of the gardens of the Petit Trianon, beyond the Rococo Style Pavillon Français, one finds two pearls of Neoclassical architecture: the Belvedere and the Temple of Love (below), built by Richard Mique in 1778. Circular in shape, it has twelve Corinthian pillars of white marble supporting a delicately sculptured architrave with plant motifs, on which rests a cupola. At the centre stands a replica of Bouchardon's statue of Love, the original now being in the Louvre.

The mill (right), is one of the rustic buildings with imitation stone painted walls, thatched roofs and lattice windows which make up Marie-Antoinette's Hameau, built by Mique in 1783 in the depths of the park of the Petit Trianon. This picturesque village on the banks of a little lake was a proper miniature farm; the dairy-cheese factory, the dovecote, the hen run and the cowsheds were grouped around the queen's house, built in two parts with big wooden arches and a covered balcony.

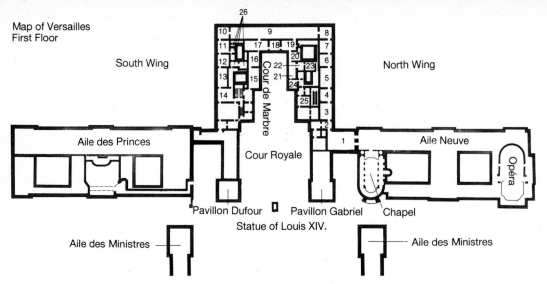

Map of Versailles
First Floor

South Wing

North Wing

26

Aile des Princes

Cour de Marbre

Cour Royale

Aile Neuve

Opéra

Pavillon Dufour

Pavillon Gabriel

Chapel

Statue of Louis XIV.

Aile des Ministres

Aile des Ministres

1 Salon d'Hercule – 2 Salon de l'Abondance – 3 Salon de Venus – 4 Salon de Diane – 5 Salon de Mars – 6 Salon de Mercure – 7 Salon d'Apollon – 8 Salon de la Guerre – 9 Hall of Mirrors – 10 Salon de la Paix – 11 Queen's Bedroom – 12 Salon des Nobles – 13 Salle du Grand Couvert – 14 Queen's Guards' Room – 15 King's Guards' Room – 16 King's Antechamber – 17 Salon de l'Oeil de Boeuf – 18 Louis XIV's Bedroom – 19 Council Chamber – 20 Louis XV's Bedroom – 21 Salle de la Pendule – 22 Antechambre des Chiens – 23 Louis XV's Dining Room – 24 Louis XV's study – 25 Louis XVI's Library – 26 The Méridienne and Petits Appartements de la Reine

Index